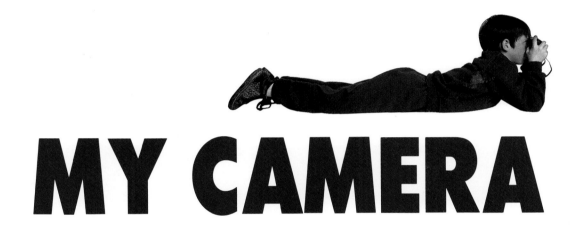

MY CAMERA

MY CAMERA

GEORGE ANCONA

CROWN PUBLISHERS, INC. • *New York*

To Addison

The pictures in this book were taken with the
simple 35-mm cameras shown, except for the
pictures of the cameras and the children holding
them. These were taken with larger-format cameras.
Both print and transparency films were used.

Published by Crown Publishers, Inc., a Random House
company, 225 Park Avenue South, New York, New York
10003

CROWN is a trademark of Crown Publishers, Inc.

Manufactured in Hong Kong

Library of Congress Cataloging-in-Publication Data
Ancona, George.
    My camera / George Ancona.
        p.   cm.
    Includes index.
    Summary: Describes the use of a simple 35-mm
camera, and gives advice and projects on composition,
lighting, action, etc.
    1. Photography—Juvenile literature.   2. 35-mm
cameras—Juvenile literature.   [1. Photography.   2.
35-mm cameras.]   I. Title.
TR149.A53   1991
771.3'2—dc20   91-2288

ISBN 0-517-58279-1 (pbk.)
        0-517-58280-5 (lib. bdg.)

First edition

10 9 8 7 6 5 4 3 2 1

CONTENTS

LOOK

at the world around you.

With your camera you
can save a part of it.

CAMERA & FILM

Your world can be photographed with a simple pocket camera. It needs batteries and is designed to use 35-mm color negative film, from which color prints are made. There are many varieties of this kind of camera to choose between.

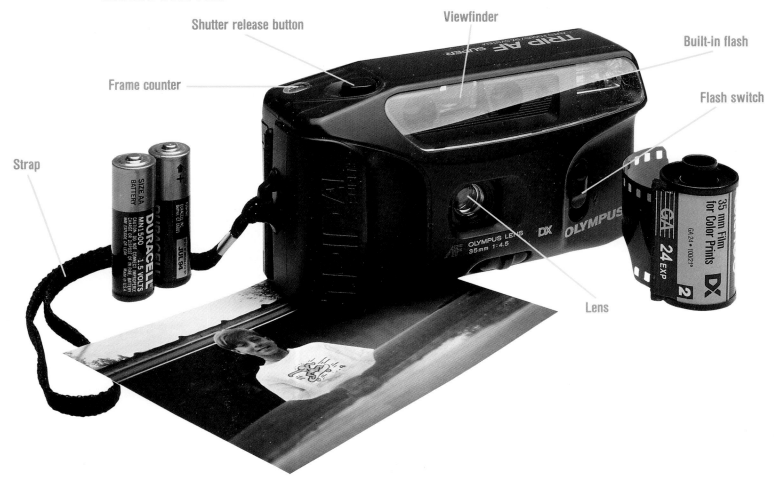

Shutter release button

Viewfinder

Built-in flash

Frame counter

Flash switch

Strap

Lens

▶ **BATTERIES** Most small cameras like this one use AA batteries. Be sure the batteries are fresh.

◀ **FILM** Rolls of 35-mm film come in three lengths—12, 24, or 36 exposures. Films also come with different "ISO numbers," which tell you how sensitive they are to light. A low number, such as ISO 100, is good for bright sunlight. A high number, such as ISO 400, is good for dark situations. Be sure to set the camera for the film you are using. Some cameras will do this automatically if you use a film with "DX" marked on the box.

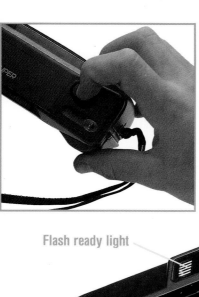

◄ **LOADING** To load the camera, open the back, insert the roll of film, and place the leader on the take-up reel. Make sure one of the holes in the film fits over a sprocket on the take-up reel. If it doesn't, the film won't move, and you will not get any pictures.

Take-up reel

Viewfinder

Flash ready light

Camera back

Sprockets

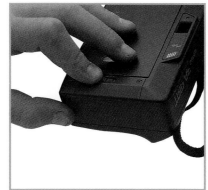

► Now close the back of the camera, making sure it snaps shut. Shoot off three frames or until the number 1 appears in the film counter window. Now there is unexposed film behind the lens, and you are ready to shoot.

◄ **FLASH** Some cameras come with a built-in flash. When there isn't enough light to take a picture, a red light appears in the viewfinder when you lightly press the shutter release button.

► Turn the flash on and then take the picture. Some cameras will automatically shoot the flash when the scene is too dark.

◄ **WHEN THE FILM IS FINISHED…**
The camera stops taking pictures when you reach the end of the roll of the film. (Check the film counter to be sure.) Now you can rewind the film. Some cameras do this automatically.

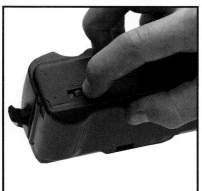

► Open the back, take out the film, and take it to the store to be developed.

Before you begin to take pictures, sli[de] your hand through the wrist strap of the camera. This prevents the camer[a] from accidentally dropping to the ground. Hold it in both hands with your right index finger on the shutte[r] release button.

◄ Holding the camera horizontally will produce a horizontal picture.

READY TO SHOOT

Bring the camera up to your eye so that you can look through the viewfinder. Steady the camera with your left hand, making sure that none of your fingers are covering the lens, viewfinder, or the built-in flash. Push the shutter release button with an even pressure so that the camera doesn't jiggle.

► Turning the camera so that it is vertical will give you a vertical picture.

TAKING A PICTURE

Move around until you have the
person or object framed the way you
like it in the viewfinder. Don't stand
any closer to your subject than 4 feet
3 inches (1.3 meters)—the length of
a broomstick—or the subject will be
fuzzy, or *out of focus*. When you
press the shutter release button
halfway down, an autofocus
camera will focus on the subject
in the middle of the frame. Press
the button all the way down to
take the picture.

◀ Taking a picture a broom's length (about 4 feet 3 inches) from the subject will give you a closeup.

◀ When you move farther away to include more of the background, the picture becomes a medium shot.

◀ When you stand very far away from what you are photographing, it's called a long shot.

LIGHT

From sunrise to sunset, a day provides all kinds of light to take pictures by. With a simple camera the best results are achieved by having the sun behind one shoulder. This keeps the sun at an angle so that the person you are photographing doesn't squint into the direct sunlight. It also keeps the sun out of the lens of the camera, which causes flares in the picture.

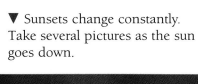
▼ Sunsets change constantly. Take several pictures as the sun goes down.

▲ Pointing the camera into the sun will produce silhouettes. It can also emphasize the color of translucent objects, such as the kite in this picture.

▼ Open shade such as that beneath trees creates a soft light that is flattering for pictures of people.

▲ Light takes on the color of the surfaces it hits or bounces off of. It gives this picture a warm tone.

FLASH!

When your camera warns you that you need to use the flash, try not to be any closer than 15 feet from your subject, or the flash will be too bright and the picture overexposed. When using sensitive films with high ISO numbers you must stand even farther away.

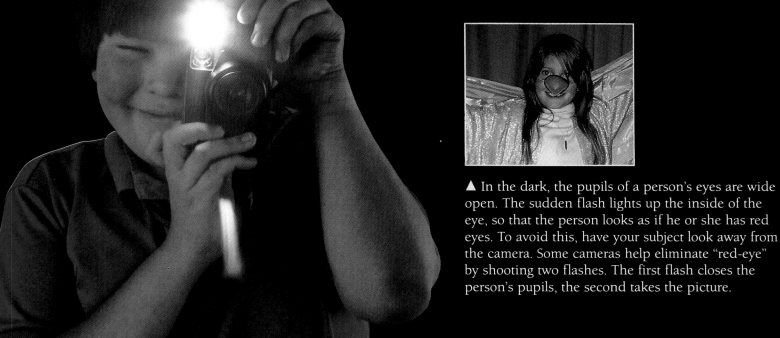

▲ In the dark, the pupils of a person's eyes are wide open. The sudden flash lights up the inside of the eye, so that the person looks as if he or she has red eyes. To avoid this, have your subject look away from the camera. Some cameras help eliminate "red-eye" by shooting two flashes. The first flash closes the person's pupils, the second takes the picture.

◄ A flash allows you to shoot indoors and stop the action or movement of your subject.

▼ Used out of doors on a bright sunny day, a flash lightens shadows and gives highlights to a person's eyes.

▼ Having the flash ready is good for capturing the arrival of visitors.

▲ Using a flash indoors next to a window helps to equalize the exposure between the scene outside and the scene inside. But be careful not to shoot directly into the window, since that will produce a reflection of the flash in your picture.

POSED...

There are many ways to photograph people. Friends and family can pose for you by standing still. But some of the best pictures happen when you shoot while they are doing something else and not expecting you to photograph them.

OR UNPOSED?

▲ The way most folks see the world…straight ahead.

◄ …But look up and you will find clouds, trees, birds, or tall buildings.

IT'S ALL A POINT OF VIEW

The camera is a tool for exploring the world, and trying different angles can result in exciting pictures. A photograph can reveal something new in an ordinary subject simply because of the way it was seen by the photographer. Shooting from different angles—straight, low, up, down, or tilted—can create unusual pictures.

▲ Looking down from above…

◀ or bringing the camera down to ground level…

can open up a new view of things.

▼ A bend in your body will place the world at an angle and can produce an unsettling view in the picture.

GETTING CLOSER

Some cameras permit you to get closer than a broomstick length and still keep your subject in focus. These are cameras with a *tele* or *macro* lens. When a button on the camera is pressed, the front of the lens moves out, allowing you to get as close as 2 feet from the subject. This is good for portraits and for shooting smaller objects.

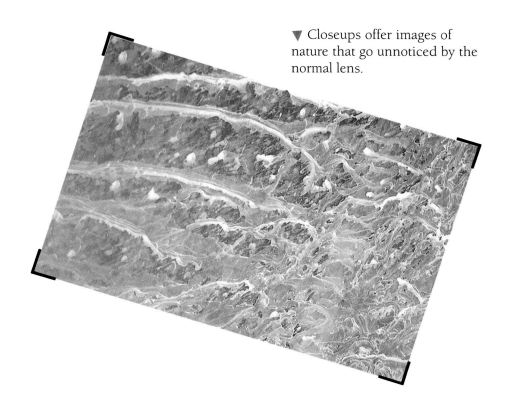

▼ Closeups offer images of nature that go unnoticed by the normal lens.

◀ Using the tele mode on your camera lets you get close to a large subject. If shooting on the shadow side, use the flash.

▼ Taking pictures of your toy friends is easier if you use a camera with a tele or closeup mode. Using the flash will lighten the shadows, but don't get too close because the flash will wash out the image.

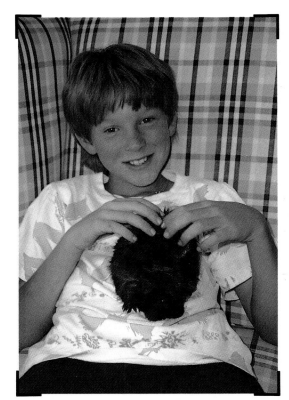

▲ If your subject is small, then put it together with someone who will fill out the picture.

MY BEST FRIEND

Each person in the world is unique. By spending time taking pictures of a friend, you can explore the many moods and doings of someone who is close to you. The camera becomes a way of getting to know a person even better.

▼ Without a flash, window light gives a natural look to pictures taken indoors.

▲ An early start to a day with your best friend. Use a flash for the indoor pictures.

▲ A silhouette of your friend's profile against the window makes a dramatic portrait.

▼ A portrait of your best friend with her mother brings a little more of your friend's world into the picture.

▼ Outside you can use the sun to light the edge of your subject while shooting on the shadowy side.

PETS

Animals are difficult to photograph since they may not do what you would like them to do. Small pets are particularly hard to shoot because the camera cannot get close enough. Including a person can provide scale to show how small the animals really are—and the person can hold them if necessary! A closeup of a larger animal can be another way of seeing it.

◄ There now—you can keep the cats still by having your sister hold them. Having a person in the picture also provides a sense of scale.

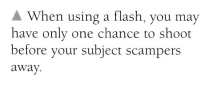

▲ This is about the closest you can get to a small subject. The flash will stop the movement.

▲ When using a flash, you may have only one chance to shoot before your subject scampers away.

▶ It is helpful to have someone distract your horse's attention to keep it from moving.

▶ When panning, try to move the camera at the same speed as the subject.

It is not easy to try to capture action with a simple camera that has a slow-moving shutter. It helps to "pan," or move with a fast-moving subject. This will blur the background but keep the figure fairly sharp. Waiting for the action to peak or an athlete to change direction is also a good way to shoot. That is the moment when the action slows up a bit.

ACTION PICTURES

▲ Move with the subject. If there's a pause in the action—shoot.

▲ In low light, pan with the subject. The background will blur, and the subject will be sharper.

▲ With plenty of light on the subject—or a light background—the subject will be less blurred.

◀ Watch for a moment when the subject changes direction. That's when the movement slows down.

▲ Wait for the action to peak, then press the button.

STILL PICTURES

A photograph is created by the person looking through the viewfinder of a camera. Everything outside of the frame disappears, and you see only how light falls on the subject. Simple, ordinary things become fascinating and beautiful. A shadow can describe so much. And a picture can concentrate the power of color.

To make the correct exposure, a simple camera measures the light in the center of the frame. To get a nice dark shadow like this one, the exposure must be correct for the light area. Point the camera to the light area, press the shutter release button halfway to record the exposure, and hold it while you compose the picture. Then press the shutter release button.

Simple objects can tell a great deal about their owners.

Don't be afraid to shoot in the shade. If there is enough light, the camera will shoot. If there isn't, use the flash.

Still lifes are good for practice and for getting to know what your camera can do. Remember not to get closer to your subject than your camera will allow, otherwise your image will not be sharp.

▲ Try to take pictures that tell a story. Here is the beginning: the whole family loading up for a day at the beach.

▲ On a bright sunny day, use the flash to lighten, or fill in the shadows.

Photographs can preserve the good times that we have. A day at the beach is a chance to take pictures of things you don't ordinarily see or do. But there are things to be careful of. The camera should not lie in the hot sun. When not being used, it should be kept away from sand and salt water in a waterproof bag in the shade.

OFF TO THE BEACH

▲ While close to the water, keep one eye on the incoming waves. Salt water on the camera should be wiped off with a cloth moistened with fresh water.

▲ The unposed, unsuspecting parent.

▲ Take the camera with you on a walk along the shore and discover unexpected pictures.

▲ Through your pictures, the day will be remembered for many years to come.

▲ Whether it is a city skyline or the Grand Canyon, it is impossible to take only one picture of a big expanse like this. So take a series of pictures and put them together in a montage. Concentrate each frame on a light or dark area. This way, each individual section of the montage will be correctly exposed. You will then be able to see details in the shadows and highlights that you would not see in a single photograph.

After matching up the connecting sections, paste the prints onto a sheet of cardboard or paper with rubber cement.

A TRIP

▶ From beginning to end, photographs of a trip make a good story to show to those who stayed at home...and preserve the memory of a wonderful experience.

There's no need to be frustrated by how little the camera frame can see of a huge landscape. Simply take a series of pictures and paste them together to make a montage. Of course, pictures of your friends and the sites along the way will tell the full story.

All those pictures of your mom, dad, brother, sister, grandpa, grandma, cousins, uncles, and aunts belong in the family album. It can grow along with the family. Perhaps you can become the family photographer and keep the album, adding to it from one year to the next. Writing down the dates and the names will help you to identify everyone in later years.

A FAMILY ALBUM

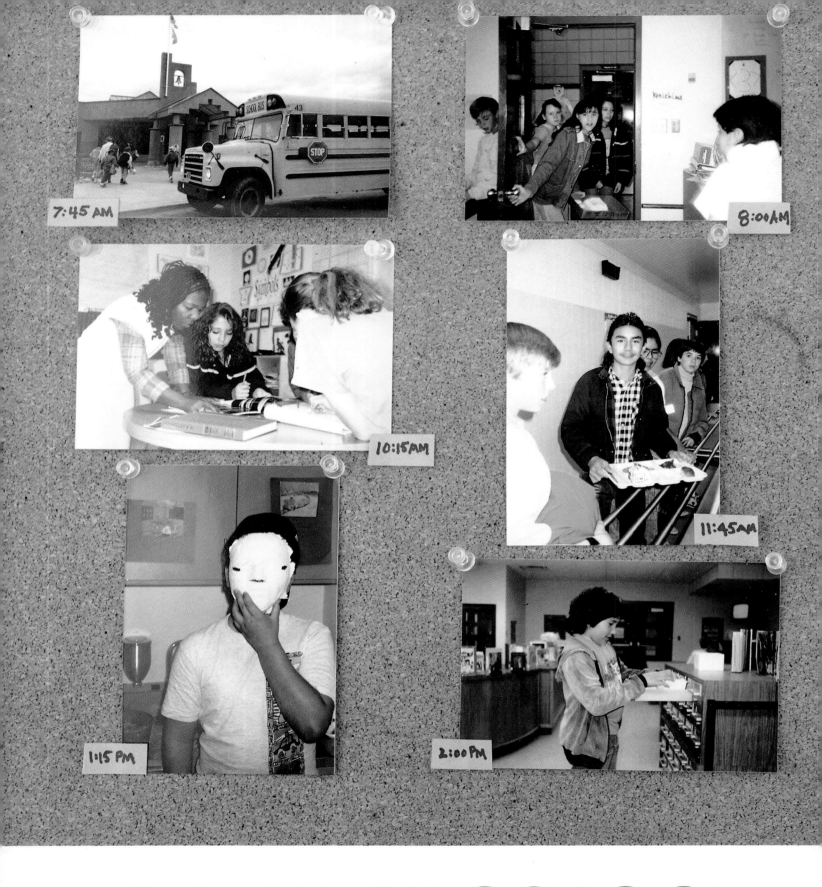

7:45 AM

8:00 AM

10:15 AM

11:45 AM

1:15 PM

2:00 PM

A DAY AT SCHOOL

8:45AM

9:30AM

12:36 PM

12:30 PM

2:30 P.M

3:00 PM

Take a camera to school to show the many activities that make up a day. The kids in your class, your teacher, and different activities can be photographed, and the prints put on a bulletin board for all to see.

A SPECIAL EVENT

The big event of the year, such as the school play, can be documented for an exhibit, the school yearbook, or your own photo album. It is important to show the rehearsals as well as the event itself. It is the variety that makes a series of pictures describe the event.

MAKING A BOOK

A series of photographs can tell a story. Arranging a picture story in the form of a book preserves the pictures and makes an interesting presentation.

WRITE Stories can be told with pictures alone or with a combination of pictures and words. A good way to start is to write down your story ideas. Your thoughts don't have to be in order at first. You can put them in order later.

PLAN   Since film is expensive, it is better to plan out what you are going to shoot for your book before you start. By using a series of small rectangles—called "thumbnail sketches"—to represent each page, you can plan the beginning, middle, and end of your book. This will give you a "shooting script."

SHOOT   Now you can go out and take pictures for your story. With your shooting script, you know exactly how each picture will be used and what it has to show.

EDIT   Since a photographer takes more than one picture when trying to capture an idea, the prints must be edited when they return from the laboratory. Only the picture that best expresses the book's idea is used.

CUT   Photographs are rectangular and all the same size when they are returned from the laboratory. They can be used this way or cut up into shapes, or the figures can be silhouetted.

PASTE   Use rubber cement or glue to paste the pictures onto the pages of the book.

LETTERING   The story can be lettered under, over, or around the pictures. Drawings can be combined with the photographs. The lettering can be in black or colored inks.

THE FINISHED BOOK   There are several ways of binding the pages of a book. They can stitched together on a sewing machine or stapled, or holes can be punched and ring binders used. The covers can be made of cardboard wrapped with colored paper and pasted or taped together. Your finished book is a wonderful way to share your thoughts and ideas. They can be saved and used for a lifetime.

HOW A CAMERA WORKS

A camera is a lightproof box that holds film behind a lens. When light is allowed to enter the box through the lens, an image is recorded on the film.

Between the lens and the film is an *iris diaphragm,* a series of blades that form an *aperture,* or hole. The blades can be moved to vary the size of the aperture, which controls the amount of light that reaches the film.

Behind the diaphragm is the *shutter,* a blade that opens and closes to allow light to reach the film. The length of time that the shutter is open is called the *shutter speed.* The combination of the shutter speed and the size of the aperture determines the exposure of the film to light. If too little light reaches the film, the picture will be dark, or *underexposed.* If too much light reaches the film, the picture will be light, or *overexposed.*

The simplest cameras have a fixed aperture and fixed shutter speed. In automatic cameras, a built-in *light meter* measures the amount of light entering the camera, and controls the size of the aperture and the shutter speed to allow the right amount of light to reach the film. Films with low ISO numbers (ISO 100) are called slower films and require more light than faster films, which have high ISO numbers (ISO 400). That's why faster films are used for action pictures and low-light situations. If the light is too low for the film, the light meter in an automatic camera will indicate that the flash is needed.

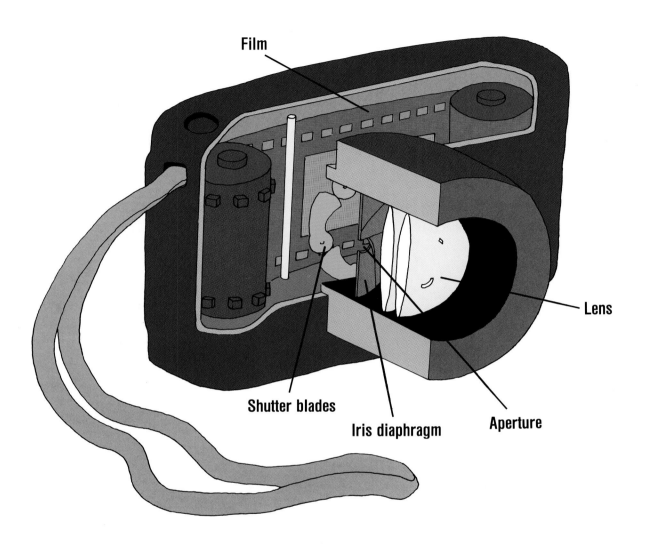

Film

Lens

Shutter blades

Iris diaphragm

Aperture

To *focus,* or make an image sharp, the lens moves toward or away from the film. Autofocus cameras do this automatically when the shutter release button is lightly pressed. Other cameras are focused by hand by turning the lens. The simplest cameras have fixed focus, which limits how close you can get to the subject.

This book would not have been possible without the contributions of the following photographers: Pablo Ancona, Jesse Belcher, the Krents, Bruce Haverkos, Joaquin Montoya, Misty Rose Morrow, David Rahr, Nina Serrano, Micah Sakiestewa Sze.

Thanks to the Olympus Corporation for their contribution of an Olympus Trip AF camera.

My thanks also go to all the people who helped in the making of this book; the faculty and students of the Santa Fe Waldorf School; Theresa Gonzalez Sadler, the principal, and Lydia Osorgin and her sixth-grade class from the Turquoise Trail School in Santa Fe, New Mexico; Peter Wilson, headmaster, and students of the Old Trail School in Bath, Ohio; Elijah Bryant, Nikolai Armendariz, and the Serrano Family.